I will not kick my friends

I will not kick my friends

Kathleen Winter

ELIXIR PRESS   DENVER, COLORADO

I WILL NOT KICK MY FRIENDS. Copyright © 2018 by Kathleen Winter. All rights reserved. Printed in the United States of America. For information, address Elixir Press, PO Box 27029, Denver, CO 80227.

www.elixirpress.com

Book design by Steven Seighman
Cover photo © The Estate of Garry Winogrand, courtesy of Fraenkel Gallery, San Francisco

Library of Congress Cataloging-in-Publication Data
Names: Winter, Kathleen, 1961- author.Title: I will not kick my friends : poems / Kathleen Winter.
Description: Denver, Colorado : Elixir Press, [2018] | Includes   bibliographical references
and index.Identifiers: LCCN 2017031031 | ISBN 9781932418651 (alk. paper)Classification:
LCC PS3623.I6724 A6 2018 | DDC 811/.6--dc23 LC recordavailable at https://lccn.loc.
gov/2017031031

10   9   8   7   6   5   4   3   2   1

Allison Moseley & Eva Valencia—
for you, dear friends

Table of Contents

. . . I still felt it, the substance of the soul, the libidinal terrible whatever.
—DARCIE DENNIGAN

Introduction

To enter the world of Kathleen Winter's dynamic second collection, *I will not kick my friends*, is to embark on a vertiginous pilgrimage through our post-post modern world where the comforting notion of a unified self has been shattered and canny wayfarers engage in a perilous reconstruction:

> We slip through our lives on the almost random path
> a raindrop rides down a windshield.
>
> The night of the cyclone, my neighbor stayed on for another glass of wine,
> side-stepped death when a sycamore smashed his bedroom.
>
> First husbands, wives, are unselected to give rise
> to meet and right varieties, the possibility of onwards.
>
> So to do is atheist, is human: we cherish what scraps of liturgy
> we still hear in our inner ears.

The here and now, as Winter's verse attests, is a space where the accidents of fate and the beauty of the natural world exist in counterpoint; thus, survival within it seems chancy, an unexpected miracle. Still, there's a necessary grace in embracing the Darwinian principles of nature, in learning one's place in a universe where even the pain of broken marriages is premeditated and purposeful. A couple may be seen as a grafting to be hybridized in hopes of better succession, a choice maneuver toward the more robust future that this poet terms "the possibility of onwards."

A key part of what propels possibility, in Winter's vision, is the secular liturgy of conversation, whether this takes place via a private (and often explosive) exchange between lovers, friends, and neighbors ("two mothers talked & laughed so long their boiling bottled formula/ blew up/ /glass glittering a kitchen") or, as is more frequent throughout this collection, an exchange of ideas.

Winter's poems commune with a host of literary and artistic antecedents, calling on familiar luminaries (Rimbaud, Cendrars, Follain, Stevens, Mansfield, Plath, and others,) as well as contemporaries like Susanna Coffey and Brenda Hillman, whose conference talks spark two of Winter's compelling collages ("Letter from Iceland" and "I will not kick my friends," respectively)—artists whose work, to varying degrees, embodies some form of political resistance and shares a commitment to authenticity.

Equally compelling is Winter's affinity with surrealist artists like Remedios Varo, whose Bosch-like canvases reflected her feminist vision and interest in scientific discovery. In "Plague Saints," Winter situates the painter in her studio, staring "down a microscope/ to make a study of the vectors of disease/ surreal as her elaborate oils," while also reminding us of the historical cataclysms that formed the backdrop of Varo's work—"the Spanish Civil War, Nazi occupation of Paris,/ events that drove the painter to Mexico and Venezuela"— factors that no doubt shaped the deeply mystical iconography of her oeuvre. Winter's crisp imagery both reveals their kinship and brings that beautifully spectral vision alive:

> The sensorium holds so much more than eggs, salt, bread and matches.
> Even what's common contains its secret, overlooked exaggerations—
> the Mercator Projection's infinitely long poles.
>
> Under glass, atoms of illness strike us
> with their beauty. Magnified cross-cuts of bone
> reveal landscapes of arctic lace.

Throughout the collection, the lives and art of philosophers, poets, and other artists (like Varo) in whom Winter finds inspiration, form a latter-day canon of visionary healers along the line of medieval "plague saints"—welcome intercessors during times of pestilence:

> Plague saints are not afraid to touch the dying.
> The saints conceive all time as present, no matter
> they were slain millennia ago.

Beyond metaphorical resonance, Winter finds solace in the unconventional expression of faith and art's triumphant transcendence of a particular historical present:

> Varo refuses Mass, yet saints grace these canvases—
> thickets of crystalline branches bear her regrets
> into their quivering music.

Winter's poems track the movement of a pilgrim soul and provide a lively travelogue through European galleries and museums familiar on the tourist track. Yet these are no static renderings of a catalogue seen in transit and recollected from afar. Instead, Winter's fluid lines unfold a lively and quizzical line of questioning about human perception and her own artistic ambition:

> what does it matter
> if the center isn't fixed—alteration
>
> is one way to make things fit
>
> to paint my portrait I'll translate
> myself to water   not a body

She writes, too, with an eye toward the way the feminine has been conventionally enshrined in literature and art, interrogating inherited forms and genres. "Garden Party Reprise" is an exquisitely chilling pantoum whose formal constraints underscore the restrictive nature of early twentieth century conventional gender roles. In "Spy," the poet captures the

thrilling pace of intrigue ("Tinker, tailor,/ entrails in the bathwater...")
while musing on the genre's darker currents and audience complicity ("I'd
survive in this world/ just five minutes. So why/ do I pay for terror?"). At
the same time, poems like "Noir" and "Nouvelle Vague" offer captivating
takes on the Eden myth ("god this garden bores me./ Only one man, and
the animals/ talk too much..."), wryly acknowledging the seductive nature
of archetype and the desire to remake traditional plotlines:

> Even Adam might be
> handsome if I could get him
> into a turtleneck, a Citroën coupe.
> That man is still incredibly naïve.
> If I could stop his grinning
> long enough to smoke a cigarette
> I'd tell him about Sartre.
> Stare into his eyes
> until this shrubbery
> seemed only a strange dream.

Though serious in their intent, Winter's poems are not without dis-
cerning wit. In "Screenplay for a Homemade Movie," the poet muses on
contemporary divorce in suburban settings. The fact that a "cousin & his
wife married/ their next door neighbors," she suggests, is revelatory—such
events are "as romantic as Pleasanton gets." Behind this appealing narra-
tive, Winter observes a stranger physics at work:

> Like bowling alley mechanics:
> after the smashes, everything set up again—
> same houses, different spouses.

Sparkling, satirical, and highly referential, Winter's poems offer deep
rewards. They consistently resist scholarly insularity, and the overall effect
is a refreshingly choral, intoxicating verse.

—*Jane Satterfield*

I will not kick my friends

Noir

All the animals in the garden
knew the score: Rat knew,
Gnu knew, even Gnat
knew Snake was telling me
what to do. Snake whispered,
he lisped; he said I was
an ignorant bimbo, he said
I was expendable, a rib.
Snake was a reptile
and he was a pigeon, too.
He offered me the apple—
what could I do?

Nouvelle Vague

. . . god this garden bores me.
Only one man, and the animals
talk too much. No café tables
beneath the tree canopy,
not a single boutique.
I could bear the tedium
till yesterday, when the snake
slipped me some pomegranate seeds.
Now I see how sweet the ocelot
would look as a coat,
the snake himself would make
a smashing jacket.
Even Adam might be
handsome if I could get him
into a turtleneck, a Citroën coupe.
That man is still incredibly naïve.
If I could stop his grinning
long enough to smoke a cigarette
I'd tell him about Sartre.
Stare into his eyes
until this shrubbery
seemed only a strange dream.

Spy

Thrillers leaf-shake my limbs:
if you're my lover I'll clutch you.
Through the opening hour,
synapses stutter. Tinker, tailor,
entrails in the bathwater.
The director sets hard action
in silence. See him
smash her face
against glass, twice,
across the night canyon
of a Budapest street.
No pop songs to assault
credibility, no orchestration
as the fragile shatter.
I'd survive in this world
just five minutes. So why
do I pay for terror?
There is, must be, some pleasure
to feel my pulse accelerate,
shiver and wonder if the man
we trusted to deliver
is leading us, in kitten heels
on cobblestones, sleek
in a Courrèges suit, to coffee
or forever.

Bad Blood II –a Review

after Arthur Rimbaud

Literally, a horror. I've known clumsiness in flayers
& scorchers but theirs I find barbarous ineptitude, a sacrilege
to the trade. All hands, liars; sons of good families, but in fighting,
lazier than the toad.

The master criminals' blue-white hair & Gallic domesticity,
their idolatry, sickens me: I don't care. Narrow skulls, disgusting
clothes, what beasts! Honestly, families like that owe everything
to lust—magnanimous plough—using the body for a living,
butter on the tongue.

But oh! my pen is intact: perfidious indolence is grass.
Only a base age of beggars, like my own, could declare this castration
magnificent. I never shall.

a port in air

bruised
by dead icy father
Hollywood suppers
in a voice rich
as peach
just past prime
he corrects the Fresh Air host
without humility
savoring sound of himself
saying *Timing is Everything*
for path of the bullet
bypassing barely his heart
rapt in instinct of contraction
the bullet shattering
mere ribs to reach
regenerating liver
so decades later he can say
(without humor)
Who else here
has taken lead?
singular character
in the Western
he never stops acting
he makes the air
surround him
empty as an empty
jar

Screenplay for a Homemade Movie

My cousin & his wife married
their next-door neighbors.
This is as romantic as Pleasanton gets.
First each other,
then after eight years, a couple of divorces.
Like bowling alley mechanics:
after the smashes, everything set up again—
same houses, different spouses.
For a while it was awkward
at the grocery, at the hardware store,
but my cousin's wife is happier now
—she's a whole different person.
Pleasanton's best had hives
about the hanky-panky
but after the neighbors remarried
the town forgot the starting lineup,
gave its blessing to two sets of newlyweds.
My cousin's next-door neighbor's wife
is happier now. She hears my cousin
only if two windows are open
& the ravens pause in bringing on
the triumph of their small, shrill song.

saint of disobedient girls

with my soon-to-be former stepsister I sped toward the Skellig
housing a sizeable gannetry snowy in June's eternal afternoon

birds bright as 40,000 lightbulbs on a blinding white backdrop
of their own dried shit, plastered on serrated flanks
of a triangular peak plunked in Atlantic's ecstatic blue

Unesco World Heritage said Leave those birds alone!
but we were avid fans, found gannets four times fresher
than the monks of Skellig Michael & all Ireland's revolutionaries, Romans,
Celts

we couldn't care less about Luke Skywalker
or his crew rigging the archangel's rock next door for sound

we docked, we disembarked, we scaled Little Skellig's layers—
steep, stepless & without a restroom, lighthouse, postcard kiosk, helicopter pad

if we were disobedient, our actions each were sanctioned by our saint
her force fiercer than globalization, slicker than lobbyists, more glamorous
than Hollywood, more tempting than revenge

we saw those birds up close

we took amazing shots with just our Hello Kitty-covered phones

when we got home we nagged our parents, who at the time were splitting up,
about the splendid gannetry where every steadfast pair preens
in the catbird seat of paradox—(semi-) protected
& yet wild &
free

The imagined comes from the imagined.

—*Brenda Hillman*

glamour

for Sylvia Plath

toofastblackcar
        too fast

to be replaced by one so much
more beautiful   of course it killed her

       (what you get, for trying to be a cupcake)

let sparrows harry the raptor
let murderess dip her blade

of grass in perfume

       every twisting strand of hair

   a rope could save
      or hang you

we have some things to work on mentally—

   *of cours*e : a phrase we usually won't need

clearly generally : iceberg lettuce of the language

Broadway star hawked coffee in recovery

     of course in general coffee makes you

pretty   meet me at the Church of the Immaculate
Virgin

corner of Beaver and Cherry

toofastblackcar!

Flagstaff, I told you so   if you're rich
you don't have to be friendly

is anything better now?

at the time she died, even the literati
thought arugula was a weed

The Garden Party

Her in her hat, him in his casket,
both covered with daisies.

Too many flowers   in some houses   banked callas

    given an accident outside the gates.

          Is there a way to eat cake without feeling,
      without feeling greedy?

The band under an awning
and women on platforms again:

      so many inches of wishing
          to be slender   see further   be seen.

Order-taker, a carter,
      his horse jumps away from the engine.

Taste the bourbon vanilla, the egg.

        We're eating leaves of grass
      in sandwiches, suffering
        creatures in the corners of our eyes:

      children in cheap crepe   like miniature servants.

* * * *

He hummed the same jingle
    always when he walked with them,

his hands on the backs
of their necks.

Scent of his sweat
clean as bread.

Strenuous to lift, to carry,
strenuous to bend and twist. Strenuous incense
masking morbidity, strenuous to use
the muscle, memory.

Strenuous to break
from a dream of him covered
with shaving soap

saying my
name in his near-
sighted eyes.

after Katherine Mansfield

Rosemary, Pansies, Fennel, Columbines

Meanwhile, birds are singing in their Greek;
      trees stir and chirrup, the darker veins
   through buttery leaves like maps
      of the routes of medicines
  or poison. I am not insane
yet I am out of breath waiting for him to be out of breath:
      waiting for the curtain, the rupture,

tactile fact. To be compelled into acceptance,
      prone among blossoms, carried by water warm as a body
   away but not drowning, mixed with lace spangle
      of light on the leaves and the river,
  one with a scatter of flowers; not drowning, not dying
but entrained—a sleeper who knows she is flying
      and does not question.

in & out of the Main Branch elevator

reckoning in books the things I love
people who make & love them

reclaiming a relation out loud
        or in a dream

remaking the ultrasound
into a healthy habit   losing my wallet

taking the elevator is a chance
to talk about panic with a friend for two seconds

        three   heart's murmur quickening

my claustrophobia a joke in the light
of its naming   reverberating in the metal
six-sided cell plunging down

to the right place

at the right speed

so often things work out
okay   you get a call saying *normal*

the rest of the day you feel it
in your gut: the lack of the Loch Ness

Monster   this sense of the sky as a liquid
opal   spreading luck in all directions—

Picture Book of Saints

for Eva & Tom

Saint of Do No Harm   Saint of Flow   Saint of
Survival Space Dog Saint   Portrait of a Lady Saint
Saint of Stairway Walks in San Francisco   Saint of
the Sensuous   Saint Hamlet   Saint of the Ghost of
Poe   Radical Saint   Saint Ariel   Saint of Thieves
Saint of Service   Housekeeping Saint   Saint of Guns
Germs & Steel   Mysteries of the Saint   Saint of
Sound & Fury   Saint of Meta-mathematics   Dream
Song Saint   Vertigo Saint   The Saint Speaks   Saint
of the Elizabethan World Picture   Letters to a
Young Saint   Saint of the Bluest Eye   Saint of the
Information   Dreamland Saint   Plague Saint   Saint
of the Face of Spain   Highly Sensitive Saint   Saint
of Gorgeous Nothings   Saint of Civilization and Its
Discontents   Saint of Illuminations   Flight of the
Raven Saint   Blue Flower Saint   Saint of Maps of
the Imagination   Saint of the Unswept Path   Saint
with Something for the Pain   Saint of Thirteen
Clocks   Saint in the Mecca   Melancholy Saint   Saint
of the Garden Party   The Complete Saint   A
Children's Saint   Saint of Labor   Saint of How to Live
Saint of How to Leave

Portrait of a Lady

The sea's a glittering negative, like a Henry James sentence, of the sky.

There's an economy of understanding: intelligent, presumptuous,
sometimes we spend a fortune in injury to buy enlightenment,

Isabel Archer's mistake even more painful on the second reading.

Yet we drive to be unblinded, shorn like monks, or athletes pretending
to be humble. Who could be humble with souls so quick and willful.

Dazzling is for James a perilous word—

beware of dazzlers in summer's pacific afternoon,
sand blanketed with bodies, teens with boards

like giants' tongues. Every last wave surges in muddy, heavy with gift.

Under the surface, great whites watch as oceans fill up with plastic.
More plastic soon than fish, if seers are genuine.

Isabel held *to her ear all day a shell of the sea of the past.*

The shark's body is pure, is perfect, claims a scientist.

But what hazard to assume this,
or any animal, could rule the land or sea.

Blue Pacific, finite lady, who could mistake you for an instrument—
possession or lifeless thing to be commanded.

Without humility, can we imagine anything but ending?

I will not kick my friends

start where the tunnel ends:
the you in the song is me
        but I stole generously from your story

they were young in a dull
              hot
              town

       yet   that Spring   all the fruit froze in the Valley

two mothers talked & laughed so long their boiling bottled formula
blew up
           glass glittering a kitchen

           now they're fiends (heh heh) for forty years

vintage Mercedes rag-top model—
vanilla enamel
            evil wheel(s):
                      fate Faulkner imagines for Caddy

stamps
   berries
  yeast
          what's childhood
            to a woman who has everything?

a beetle wanders with authority
inside the windshield   waves a leg

      Stravinsky's brass section
      jeered at him until their brains

                changed   ran riot into

Beauty—do you wonder why you're literately ill?

      (her head hasn't flown off
       for months)

         girls were scolded to sit still
            but every child should have a wingchair

once, Greg was a boy
so: presidential

      on the beach tonight   I see his teeth
      from twenty feet

        fork & knife X his plate to prove
    he's a pirate

if you think
you have
a unified
self
      (that ringing isn't supposed to be here)

Judge made you write it down
a hundred times   I'll turn my phone off

in the courtroom
     say something   indelible

        you don't listen to your brain too much

the longer you go   the faster it went
sayitagain

say sound a shape speed liquefies

say sight a white mustache on sister's lip

fish

 lemons

 ice

     our eyelid aprons lead

         towards night

   sax

  jasmine

   thyme

how much do I love you

   I will not kick my friends

Your deadpan

delivery kills me.
Run a knife past
scorched margins in a Pyrex
square on the counter,

Greensleeves dangling
from a banjo.

The notes span centuries,
to a mind melancholy
as mine.

Scars like spider lines
draped this mantilla on my brain.

In her self-portrait at a Bronx museum,
the artist's shawl of long black hair
falls thick and straight

as she cradles one shin
in spindly arms
to mimic the Madonna.

My feet, clean, bloodless,
rest on a dying dog's back
while the fire toasts your book
in my hands.

He tore the cover's Weston nude away
when he was teething.
Together again in your words,

let's consider the mental life
of the soul—as though
there were any other way
to eat this sweet darkness.

Frigorifero

The homonymy of medieval backwaters
is nothing to my solitude
as I train to be daring
pediatrician to the future.

Mama chose a strange place
to give birth.
Who am I, the human eye, to aid her?

Neither Great Dane nor rainstorm
can budge her from the deck rail,
fistful of grey will,
her beak locked shut as yet.

This morning my sea so frozen,
even Kafka's axe chips only a few flakes.
What do I care to wake up for,
let alone sit my ground to save?

My love's gone running
beneath ancient trees,
the dog circling a cave in the bed's
last warm space.

I am that white and foreign box
preserving vague savories under glass,
thick and low, humming in my corner.

Postcard 1908: Death-tropes of the Feminine

Shall never forget the spread
we didn't have.

The facts are
there are none
in the assortment
but what are really
more attractive
than this sample:

    large ones
    juicy ones

    soft ones a specialty

We're reading a long terrible novel
The Tunnel
and playing lottery
in hope of affording
a trip to the place
where time and character
cross paths:

perhaps it's the historical present,
where Henry James
himself softens up and says

The proof is in the pudding.

    instead of

The only measure of
excellence is execution.

At river's edge
the last patch of Roman Soldier
has frozen.
Already, Uncle
speaks of syruping.

Write and let us know
you are not dead.

A Day of Peace

after Jean Follain

A day of peace, the old man passing gifts to pigeons, to orioles with the coo of a long-tailed gal. Then again, attend to the juvenile voltage of night, the plain of hennaed rivulets, sweet deviant chant engraved by an agent of the world's end, post-Christ, less the nuance, the deaths, and after suave hours, bereft of grave sculptures. These times imply a future petulance. A child crosses over our path, bearing his own pigeon, its feet a bracelet—the orbit cannot be detached. Bearing that long journey, debut of a sodden season. Refusing to wait at home, the vague young girl tills with her yoke of blues.

Garden Party Reprise

The ladies wore eclipsing hats.
Familiar even to distress,
the epic strain, the brandy.
His garden was the Ne Plus Ultra,

its tale familiar even to distress,
that ignorance is bliss,
the Ne Plus Ultra,
if you like that sort of thing.

Ignorance is bliss
for the complacent visitors
who like that sort of thing.
But what if you're obsessed with class?

For a complacent visitor
sometimes gets anxious about change—
obsessed with class,
begins to greet the waiters with suspicion.

Anxious about change,
the well-heeled party guest
meets waiters with suspicion,
wondering How long will the music last?

Well-heeled, the garden party guest
conceives the sharpest question he can ask:
How long will this music last?
A married lady lingers at the fruit plate.

The sharpest question he can ask
hangs for an instant in the air—

the lady lingers at the fruit plate, eyes
the only apple.

Hanging for an instant in the air,
familiar even to distress,
only the apple marries with
the epic strain, the brandy.

after E.M.W. Tillyard

Advent

The driveway shakes her inner ear:
somebody's coming or going.
Darling of deconstruction, give her
a sweater, precious lamb, to get a thread.
Tactile satisfaction of destruction, yank
until recipient's a naked babe.
On her advent calendar some tiny doors
should not be opened. Never mind.
Pay attention to one blinking light
at treetop, murmur of her heating unit
under wool. She knows the string of cows
is from her grandmother, she spies
a painted pig from Uncle George.
Here's a rabbit made of glass,
here's a straw man to sacrifice.
What liquid in the bubble lights
boils red and anxious vertically,
what toothless grande dame
dented the teething ring's silver bell
now dangling by a thread of velvet—
ornament, memento. Demoiselle
of deconstruction, don't forget you know
how *not* to be destructive.
Con's a game of knowing for a girl
in fur muff singing Greensleeves
at the service, counting hats.
Out a door in her head, questions coming
about ghosts in trinities,
wine and table with a crush of men,
a con job. Darling, don't you think
that peacock feather hat
at the back of the chapel's full
of everlasting life, and will not perish?

Tonic

Let's fly to Dubai. It takes 68 hours.
When you get there you'll be changed
into an engineer from heaven.

You want to make thought visible so write it down
but the math's wrong.

Man of the people, he eats oatmeal
for fifteen years. What do you think will happen
if he don't?

JB, you pop into my head whenever
I'm scared a lonely.   Beneath his beard he

      handsome man made   calculations
          upside down across the board.

Back home, pieces of lettuce stain the sink with
ants and people work too hard.

The snake in the garden lives on after poisoning
visiting cattle dog   who knew
      too much.

      The only way to learn
is hard ways.

In the bathroom with blue metal
flashlight you look down into my scalp. The facts

      are smaller than they feel.

Brain makes you want to break

the rhythm in the main
                    before returning to the tonic chord.

Finny works too hard in his own sleep
            four legs running sideways, acoustical grunts.

Be at peace, my dear,
those scales will be here when you wake up.

                    Whenever scared
                    I'm lonely.

Ants make a Maltese cross in our sink.
The ceiling fan is simple
                            cinema,

solid wooden X that turns into a circle
                    you can see through
                    to the ceiling.

                    Turn the image off; we have to go
        to sleep.
                    Fly on, my engineer.
We're always at the point of no return.

. . . she blinded me with science.

—*Thomas Dolby*

Receptive Fields of Single Neurons
in the Cat's Striate Cortex

start from being driven:
cats on their pedestals of fur and bone

to striate structures of the cage

Livery say plates of limousines
delivering industrialists
to fundraisers   across a bridge

I could have gone to Detroit
but I struck out on my own
to buy a hundred-thousand-dollar horse

write-off of three legs
& half the torso

take apart a human
you have teeth   & glasses

a skull cap   plastic bag of calcium
sand

over those empty shoes see a ghost
of the body

my father
rode a bicycle before his face was permanently
gone   saved in this idea
I call my heart

* * * *

science thought it
legitimate in 1959
to flash a cat's eye
fierce with points
of light as needles
tracked the V1 region of its brain

first stage
of the visual cortex

                    we want to know
                    precisely how to see

among a trash of animals
          discovery was accident

one cat's brain excited
by straight lines
               by angles

* * * *

what does he care
          the candidate
                    a wishful type of general

for events of war
          at the levels of cells and limbs?

your panting will kill you
if they hear it

from a forest at the edge
of town you listen
as soldiers finish

your friends with knives
                    with points of light

companions:
            we have to get past being Man—

there are people so powerful
they go into war zones

and carry only cameras

Freud Before Bed

That anyone, for being Jew, should have to flee.
An airplane's boom, plume of white noise.

Freud before bed makes for mean sleep.
That scene of gone, piercing the hide—
fever in the jaws of animals.

That a man who thought so well
should have to wait so long.

Discontented with the smell of radishes,
I am no old European
but I hear you,

keen shrill train-whistle of conscience.
There is regret, an indigestion, bad translation.

There is a strict Modernism—
shadow-winged with sound—
that persists conflicted, flies from itself.

Thank you for beauty, for your love of it.
For keeping it at hand.

America, what are we doing here?
our nation is too loud
& proud—of its drained favors.

Plague Saints

Remedios Varo stares down a microscope
to make a study of the vectors of disease
surreal as her elaborate oils.

The brain is properly thought of
as a mostly closed system
says Eagleman.

Thus the Spanish Civil War, Nazi occupation of Paris,
events that drove the painter to Mexico and Venezuela,
to her grave at 58?

The sensorium holds so much more than eggs, salt, bread and matches.
Even what's common contains its secret, overlooked exaggerations—
the Mercator Projection's infinitely long poles.

Under glass, atoms of illness strike us
with their beauty. Magnified cross-cuts of bone
reveal landscapes of arctic lace.

Plague saints are not afraid to touch the dying.
The saints conceive all time as present, no matter
they were slain millennia ago.

Varo refuses Mass, yet saints grace these canvases—
thickets of crystalline branches bear her regrets
into their quivering music.

Dreamland Saint

See this saint from Dreamland slumming with us
where every limb sweats, mercury rising, fruit
baking in its bowl on the drainboard.
Polio, Ebola and fresh new diseases in desiccated Eden,
the neighborhood a locus of explosions, our nation
now the nation of murderous event, unlicensed carrying
on on on. Unexceptional, our state of war.
How does violence vibrate in her cranium tuned
to ocean, birdsong, intricate chant in caverns
of seven-second reverberation, cathedrals of empathy
whose marriages all thrive like headland redwoods
bathed in a cycle of sunlight and fog, sunlight
and fog for centuries. Dreamland saint, appear
to our electorate in Fall, replace the suits
on news screens, fill our representatives with joy,
humble, as though they could make a durable good.

Ode to a Physicist

frenzy of their friction scurries particles in motion
                makes the world
                           a problem
in the brilliant sense of somewhat
solvable

                although fierce carmine eyes of vehicles
          are operated by a force I fail

    to understand & words   my bread
           & butter   are combustible
       unstable:

     suffer is a sign   enacts pain's oscillation
       with allowance

              martyrs are allowed indefinitely
         to hang around
            as saints

        & *gentle*
        means to break a horse

Feynman reminds our eyes
are zones of brain
      grown out to meet the light—

      what might this imply
   for soul?

forever bridegroom of my body

where'd you go
          on business trips
                              to sleep?

          was it over lakes of infinitely miniscule divisions
                    that you fractured
                                        into vision?

Brownian motion inside gravestones

          is a finer version of eternal life than what I had
in mind in high school

                    so now tell me   what do people eat

          who start to understand the world?

          the teacher is a genius
of impatience

          but he wouldn't eat an animal

                    for me signs *meat*
                              & *cow*

                    remain conveniently discrete

Keep Right   Keep Right

                              intention
                              has a tiny
                              half-life

give me hagiography
& give me death

but not before a basic course in physics

we look at us with tenderness   dismay
          (H-bomb maker loves his little daughter)

what did I learn from him?

          joy is
to find a problem

Saint of Survival

...and when a slightly better variety chanced
to appear, selecting it, and so onwards.
—Charles Darwin

Survival's a hybrid of chance and desire, I think the saint said.
(She had an olive in her mouth, the storm was loud.)

We slip through our lives on the almost random path
a raindrop rides down a windshield.

The night of the cyclone, my neighbor stayed on for another glass of wine,
side-stepped death when a sycamore smashed his bedroom.

First husbands, wives, are unselected to give rise
to meet and right varieties, the possibility of onwards.

So to do is atheist, is human: we cherish what scraps of liturgy
we still hear in our inner ears.

Saint of Survival accepts anomalies, mistakes,
ambition. She's kind to kin, holds out her hand

to strangers who will grasp it.
She likes good food but isn't greedy, embraces pilgrimage, the chance-

directed outcome. Her boat, hull fashioned from two and a half
ox hides, brings her to an island seven miles from Ireland.

Birds' eggs, seal steaks, rainwater cache.
Who has perfect knowledge, who really knows the moon's age?

Enough is as good as a feast.

Highly Sensitive Saint

Pray slip your digits, elegantly thin, through these tangles
    in hundred-degree heat to seek the almost invisible
beasts, bane of grade-school students, their families,
        their family friends.

Nearly translucent, your sensitive fingers
    find them before our eyes.
We're itchy in good company: some somewhat-innocent kids,
        the ghosts of Rimbaud

& his sisters with delicate fingers,
    fastidious as tea rose breeders, gene-splicers.
Your saintly sensibility so fine, you sense the lice
        even before your fingers sink into our waves.

Like migraines sending hints to future victims,
    these bits of insect make spooky action at a distance.
Was physics always poetry, did Einstein make it so?
        Picture Albert in this situation, his frizzled halo

alive with entomology, a disregarded physicist assisting
    with her comb of microscopic tines.
Of course you're right—we needn't kill them:
        we could collect insects in envelopes to mail

to a former boss or ex, some iteration of the unforgiven.
    When our scalps & hair are clean, our gratitude will be
mathematical fact: information the universe may change
        the phase of, but can never erase.

Distortion Formulas

for Allison

I hope everything goes pretty well, at least.
Migrations of the headlong sea by bird flight,
organs of sacrificed animals, were declared
auspicious by antique Europeans.

East, believed to be the direction of Eden.

Cartographic projections are conventions of illusion,
said a man who should know he's been missed.

Against the sun, or widdershins, Saint Auspice wove
cocoonery for divinations. I hope everything goes pretty well,
at least. Migrations of the headlong sea by bird flight
were declared auspicious by antique Europeans,
and organs of sacrificed animals,
cartographic projections of the direction of Eden.

East, believed to be a convention of illusion.

Against the sun, or widdershins, Saint Auspice wove,
said a man who should know.

He's been missed. I hope everything goes
pretty well. At least migrations of the headlong
sea by bird flight, conventions of illusion,
organs of sacrificed animals believed to be directed
against the sun. Widdershins,
Saint Auspice wove.

Counterclockwise, liquid draining makes a neural shimmer.
What are wishes, but a benign fever?

Extinctions

After I trashed my hotel room
I sat down to think about dinosaurs.
I was running out of years
to imagine them hatching

on boughs, over our heads
like so many allusions,

coming into their own
as creatures of flight
& intestinal alchemy,

churning out gastrulae
for the pleasure of their heirs.

O the suavity of those stones—
beginning in utility, turning up
two hundred million years later
as amulets, as art.

Can one word be enemy of another?
I fished at myself, sunk
in the capital rubble,
sucking wounds.

All moves and jargon—
I spat out the poison
over ratatouille upholstery & the walls &
my dictionary : my mind.

I spat until my mouth was dry
& I couldn't spell the difference
between comedy & tragedy,

until I couldn't say
if I were alone in that room
or in the past with you,

trying to be released by sound.

Marché, Isle sur la Sorgue

Each lover is at the other's mercy.
How many states
and waves between us
for these attenuated
summer weeks?
By my dream's distortion
formula, the distance
is only a few seats
on a city bus,
from which I watch
a stranger
circle your wrist with her hand.
However wary
the unconscious,
in daylight, brilliant externals
of this herbous place
put me at ease,
at my own mercy.
Drifting in the market stream
of dark eyes,
sunbathed faces,
who could find a hippogriff
or serpent among the fragrant
compass roses.
In a fountain's music
fallen loose,
who would hope to hear
mathematics,
subtle architecture of the rules
we agreed to share.

Index of Lent

a self controlled
a syllabus of errors
an infallible Pope
a limit at the end of the pencil
a tender rigidity
a fragile aperture
an ill legitimate
a liquid infancy
a limpid innocence
an angel of doubt
a throes of closing
a shape note singing
a mythical ascension
millennial persuasion
and still the stars
taken with The Very Large Array

Saints of Meta-Mathematics

If the manly barber shears all men,
and also shears only those who don't shear themselves,
must he be bald?

Russell makes rules against recursion, paradox.
Principia Mathematica: his system of completeness runs without a hitch

until another genius, Gödel, proves some of math's truths
forever are unprovable.

And Turing shows that incomputable numbers outnumber
other numbers. Uncertainty lives

in any formal system, is fused with language, locked
in logic, baked into mathematics
like four and twenty blackbirds in pie.

       I don't look like who I am.

Monastery, verdigris, excelsior all fail
to prevail in Hangman, whereas
heifer unpredictably wins.

Framed in nine panels of foxed mirror glass
she squints into image:

       I can't look at who I am.
       I was introduced as a plot point in 1975

the year an undeterminable number
of elephants were killed by poachers.
Matriarchs, taken for their tusks.

It takes time to get past anything
as indispensable as youth.

Boole and other saints think it's okay to think of thinking
as a game, to think of language as an instrument of reason, material
our thoughts are made of, not just conveyed by.

Watching limbs of pine lift in the wind
      I'm thinking: What do I want now?

Constable wanted to do justice by the trees.

      The day is near as long as it will ever be.

Who has not had a troubled love affair
with stillness and walked the galleries filled
with dead and beautiful things and felt renewed.

—*Bruce Bond*

Explanation

So   long.

So be it. So be it long
and vague, even

dazzling in its vagueness—

the face of a cliff disintegrating, face of a faux
cliff art cliff white cliff

of Dover stone made by an artists' collective,

hung in a winery gallery.

High on the wall all the way to low on the wall of the high-
ceilinged gallery: white

Leviathan of fabrication,
cliff-face of polyurethane and paint appearing

to disintegrate like the figure's face
in Bacon's painting upstairs in the gallery—

vicious blur in an armchair.

No, you cannot drink here.

I would go on
but the alarm does not allow.

I would to what she said about /not/ dazzling

the dazzling implying light and crystalline implying blinding
bowed to

valorized.

In the carnivorous expanse of gemshow an infinitude of teeth

so long, a shining of prismatic knives:

new: hard: sharp: vertical:

but the alarm.

So be it.
I can't rise beyond the second floor

where Bacon's bloated figure sits and swings his polychrome
disintegrating face from side to side so fast the features blur

or else his head spins on a pole of neck

so quick the features smear and drip
becoming faceless, vague.

You tried to console me: *dazzling is tinsel*

but in my mind I see the grainy black-and-white of Tesla
under his transformer's flaming wings—
dazzling   radiant   vague

Missing in the Louvre

Invisible pictures
hang between
the masterpieces

in museums.
Ours are two
such slender centuries

exhausted by waste
graced
by emancipations.

One half of humanity
achingly
becoming recognized

as human
as human is a dark
and halting animal

ever possessive
of its own framed
place

in hallowed space.

The Grammar of Ornament

We shed slickers at the entrance,
    before woodcuts of peasants,
bare-breasted. In a downstairs hall
    Rome's muscle glows on the torsos.

Tonight the adults will dream about sex
    and the children about ice cream.
Take a right at the sarcophagus:
    carnivorous 18th Century,

your still-life of rabbit and pheasant
    is titled "The Pâté."
The museum freed a grand chandelier
    from a duchess:

rock crystal fissures
    glimmer in electric light
but imagine with candles!
    You're a servant flaming dishes

and wicks, soot snowing dusk
    upon London. This saint's feet
are painted to extremes:
    each toe has its own personality.

Between twin arcs of staircase
    aluminum Eros,
on leave from Piccadilly, streaks.
    He flings a leg back toward empire,

balances his washboard
    core over an ankle.
Outside gilded frames,
    typed cards remark dates

and makers, buying habits
    of the British middle class.
Ornaments of grapevine
    and orb, peacock feather fan,

sterling teapot shaped
    like an udder—what middle class
could afford this grammar—
    the mummy's self-satisfied smile.

Inevitable Colonials

The husband as colossus
menacing and dull,
a sigh in everything she says.

Change Your Chicken cries a sign,
the March air glowering, a chill
above the river, over boathouses.

The Gravedigger's Ball goes on
as a banner going on
a metal fence in Philadelphia

across from the museum of rocks,
the most practical form of jewelry.
Take the rock he gave her

—talking rock. It said:
(like the little triangular sign
stuck into a lemon

in Frida Kahlo's visiting still life)
I belong to a dentist
menacing and dull, with teeth

on his shingle, teeth on the shutters
of his colonial. It said: We have
the luxury of eating

thoughtlessly. It said: You cannot
touch or even ask me
for the time of day

or direction out of where
a parkway of thin trees can't hide
the view of the highway.

The road to their facility:
speed limit 27, gated entry,
identical windows, rhododendron;

the only change a change
of chicken, the only hazards
on the heart's clipped courses.

Faux Romanesque

I rivaled you in size.
We were rare and shallow.

Your groined vaulting had to be
of great height to take the weight

of our central tower. Quite thick
but with a single nave,

I bore a band of blind arcading.

Your lancet window let in
very little light.

The problem was resolved
by placing a dome on squinches.

Tending to splay the walls,
your rounded arches struck the visitor

 with simplicity.

Pointed barrel vaulting meant
my downward thrust was more direct.

No tribunes except a lintel
—ornate, preceded at times by a porch;

two flanking apsidal chapels, ambulatory
as your heart.

It usually was oven vaulted,

linked to the transept crossing.

Did I say blind arcading?

Historiated, a single nave, thick
to compensate for missing walls.

I want to believe our appearance
was of a solid mass, a quadrilobed plan

to balance the whole structure.
Austerity.

Perfection of our stone bonding.

Luxembourg Gardens

Blaise Cendrars, your unicorns, smoke and Bordeaux.
        How I grieved you after the bus left that day.
    Literally we couldn't speak
        each other's language—the lyricism of fresh loss,
    grammar as a catastrophic detour.
Sparrows scurrying the garden's gravel paths mapped
        my mind's traffic, ghost miners fossicking dead veins.

How could the sculpted lovers ignore that presence
        hovering above them, a supernatural wrath?
    We froze it in photograph, his mineral envy
        over their bodies' ignorance entwined, cosmic fist
    already falling, a mountain, a tenement collapsing.
What did you feel that afternoon? Innocence is believing
        your lover wants to know.

in the Museum of the Legion of Honor

these marble busts of famous men
are starting to look younger

you're a dancer   struggling
to get centered   are you middle class

middlebrow   middle-aged
is noon truly the center of the day

doesn't it all always change   light
to welter to heavyweight

mean or median   what does it matter
if the center isn't fixed—alteration

is one way to make things fit

to paint my portrait I'll translate
myself to water   not a body

but a medium   a state   a shimmer
—there   I'm in the corner

of your eye   fleeting   fluid
nameless shape   a glimmer

libertine   a floater—
instance of the universal rain

Maison du Général Baron Robert

The church bell next door keeps six hundred years of time.
I paint a vase beside a clock, both flat as a dancer's chest,

flat as my tone of voice, a triumph
over perspective.

Over cubist jive, passé as the conceit of him
and me. Let him be a genius, bull

in his striped shirt, the prison of his ego.
I have my desolated saints, collection of canvases,

my portraits. Watch prices at the auction houses climb—
how well his reputation ages.

My sweet blood compelled him when we met.
Now it brings on insects in the infinitely tapering evening, worshippers

that make their marks on my pale
arms, as he made his.

Letter from Iceland

*We're in the world and it's bigger than we
are—this is why landscapes tend to be small.*
—Susanna Coffey

I'm literal in the shadowbox sense
of the parlance   diffuse and ruinous bliss
I'm Empress of Laxness   I don't want
to have complex ideas about flowers

say you miss me blue times
and I'll mail you a sketch of a moth
who resembles a frog
who resembles men
on their backs   thumbs and forefingers
ringing great toes

to a pale beetle crawling my breast
is the landscape
relentlessly morphing
my fingers god-machines
promised long by the sagas

all day we remake the terrain with eyes closed
after staring at the sun
circles flame

circumferences are green
I paint pines as hair flocking God's granite

skull and the sea as his brainwaves
pretending again to be human

I work toward a small relation to the trees

Saint of Labor

I met a man a man who won't make money.
Extreme, he peels away from the medium,

like a soaked label leaving it, listener
in this space of bottomless story.

What part was real, what part imagined
is past, almost past knowing, wind of hay rising

a hundred yards in the sky, ghost coach
coursing the lake's edge on a wooden road

after May light bleeds away to sea—
eels of light, ribboning.

A thousand years later they burned
the ancient hand-made roads, dug them up

into fire, cremating how many hours,
how many lives of labor.

I watch fire tearing sunwise after dark.
This man must be still to breathe,

hear sheep bleat out to the Skellig peaks.
Long work he does to be idle,

figure how to make the sea's faces
on paper. Among visitors in ruined cottages,

we're the ones whose stained fingers
speak the same solitude.

Folk Art Elegy

We were shaped by our environment.
We were figures of goats and sheep
made out of flour paste.

I remember wood boxes we lived in then,
winged doors patterned with flowers.
Three levels unconnected by stairs,
by anything less than narrative.

The people (the artists?)
were always loading us onto trucks
that churned the dirt roads that clung
to the Andes, or staging us at a manger
within sight of the baby, or selling us
in adorable markets, painted with glaze.

Silver bird in the box of the sky
was a knife.

You were a goat
with sideways face, with only one eye
to meet the world's gaze between
wings of doors and roses.

Handmade was your claim.

Notes

Darcie Dennigan, "In the Bakery," *Madame X* (Canarium Books: 2012).

"Bad Blood II—a Review" is a found poem made from the language in Arthur Rimbaud's "Bad Blood," translated by Louise Varese in *Models of the Universe: an Anthology of the Prose Poem*, ed. Stuart Friebert and David Young (Oberlin College Press: 1995).

"A Port in Air" is in conversation with Wallace Stevens' "Anecdote of the Jar," *The Collected Poems: the Corrected Edition* (Vintage International: 2015).

Brenda Hillman, "Air in the Epic," *Pieces of Air in the Epic* (Wesleyan University Press: 2005).

Katherine Mansfield, *The Garden Party and Other Stories* (Penguin: 2008).

"Portrait of a Lady" includes an italicized phrase by Henry James from *The Portrait of a Lady* (Wordsworth Editions: 1999).

"I will not kick my friends" includes italicized text by Brenda Hillman from a lecture at the Napa Valley Writers' Conference, July 2013.

"Your deadpan" is in conversation with "Father's Famous Devastation" by Olena Kalytiak Davis, *And Her Soul Out of Nothing* (University of Wisconsin Press: 1997).

In "Frigorifero," the words "the homonymy of medieval backwaters" are quoted from Robert Fossier's *The Axe and the Oath: Ordinary Life in the Middle Ages*, trans. Lydia Cochrane (Princeton University Press: 2010). The poem refers to Franz Kafka's statement: "A book must be the ax for the frozen sea inside us."

"Postcard 1908: Death-tropes of the Feminine" includes Henry James' statement: "The only measurement of excellence is execution."

Jean Follain, *D'Apres Tout: Poems by Jean Follain*, trans. Heather McHugh, (Lockert Library of Poetry in Translation: 1982).

"Garden Party Reprise" includes language from E.M.W. Tillyard's classic, *The Elizabethan World Picture: a Study of the Idea of Order in the Age of Shakespeare, Donne and Milton* (Vintage: 1959). Thanks Norman, for sharing your library.

"Tonic" quotes John Berryman's "Dream Song 40" at "I'm scared a lonely," *The Dream Songs* (Farrar, Straus, Giroux: 1986).

Thomas Dolby, "She Blinded Me with Science," *The Golden Age of Wireless* (Venice in Peril: 1982).

"Receptive Fields of Single Neurons in the Cat's Striate Cortex" and "Plague Saints" were inspired by David Eagleman's *Incognito: the Secret Lives of the Brain* (Vintage: 2012).

"Plague Saints" and "Distortion Formulas" were inspired by Peter Turchi's *Maps of the Imagination: the Writer as Cartographer* (Trinity University Press: 2007).

The Charles Darwin epigraph for "Saint of Survival," from *On the Origin of Species*, was quoted in Jared Diamond's *Guns, Germs and Steel: the Fates of Human Societies* (Norton: 1997).

"Distortion Formulas" tracks the structure of "Who Cares About Aperture" by Olena Kalytiak Davis, *And Her Soul Out of Nothing* (University of Wisconsin Press: 1997).

"Saints of Meta-Mathematics" was inspired by James Gleick's *The Information* (Vintage: 2012).

Bruce Bond, "Wind Machine," *Gold Bee* (Southern Illinois University Press: 2016).

The epigraph for "Letter from Iceland" is a statement made by Susanna Coffey during her lecture at Vermont Studio Center, February 2006.

Acknowledgements

Many thanks for use of the cover photograph by Garry Winogrand, "El Morocco, New York, 1955".

I'm grateful to the editors of the following journals, in which these poems first appeared:

AGNI Online	"Garden Party Reprise"
Alaska Quarterly Review	"Nouvelle Vague," "The Garden Party"
American Letters & Commentary	"Folk Art Elegy," "Receptive Fields of Single Neurons in the Cat's Striate Cortex"
Anti-Poetry	"Inevitable Colonials"
Bacon Review	"Extinctions"
Barrow Street	"A Port in Air," "Frigorifero"
Bluestem	"I will not kick my friends"
Burnside Review	"Distortion Formulas"
Colorado Review	"Postcard 1908: Death-tropes of the Feminine"
Confrontation Magazine	"Saint of Disobedient Girls"
Diode Poetry Journal	"Ode to a Physicist"
Fjords Magazine Online	"Maison du Général Baron Robert"
Legal Studies Forum	"Missing in the Louvre"
Memorious	"In the Museum of the Legion of Honor," "Rosemary, Pansies, Fennel, Columbines"
Michigan Quarterly Review	"Dreamland Saint," "Saint of Survival"
Mississippi Review	"Plague Saints"
New American Writing	"Explanation," "Freud Before Bed," "Letter from Iceland"
New Statesman	"Saint of Labor"
Poetry London	"Advent"

Prelude	"Faux Romanesque"
Sentence	"A Day of Peace"
Spillway	"Spy"
The Texas Observer	"Screenplay for a Homemade Movie"
Tight	"Index of Lent"
Tin House	"Glamour," "Tonic"
Volt	"in & out of the Main Branch elevator"
Watershed Review	"Bad Blood II—a Review"
Western Humanities Review	"Portrait of a Lady"
32 Poems	"Noir," "The Grammar of Ornament"

Love to you, Greg Campbell.

Love to my family—Haidee Gerhardt Winter, Raymond C. Winter, Cathy Cummins, Allison Moseley, Paul Plath, Eva Valencia, Tom Coffeen and El Otis.

Warm thanks to the Brown Foundation; Museum of Fine Arts, Houston; and Gwen Strauss for a residency at the Dora Maar House, Ménerbes, and to the James Merrill House Committee and Lynn and Jeff Callahan. I'm deeply grateful to Michael Adams, the Texas Institute of Letters, and the University of Texas for a semester residency at the Dobie Paisano Ranch, Austin. Many thanks to Robin Carstensen, *The Switchgrass Review*, and Texas A&M University, Corpus Christi, as well as to Cill Rialaig Retreat, Ireland. These people and institutions provided support, inspiration and joy that helped make this book.

For friendship, insight and encouragement, thanks to Don Bogen, Cynthia Hogue, Norman Dubie, John Johnson, Greg Mahrer, Krysia Zaroda, Jodi Hottel, Kathryn Nuernberger, Hannah Sanghee Park, Julia Lingys, John Carlisle, Sophia Park, Tim Gray, Kurt Heinzelman, Susan Terris, George David Clark, and Alberto Ríos

To Dana Curtis and Elixir Press, huge gratitude, and the same to Jane Satterfield for selecting this manuscript for the 17th Annual Elixir Press Award.

TITLES FROM ELIXIR PRESS

POETRY

Circassian Girl by Michelle Mitchell-Foust

Imago Mundi by Michelle Mitchell-Foust

Distance From Birth by Tracy Philpot

Original White Animals by Tracy Philpot

Flow Blue by Sarah Kennedy

A Witch's Dictionary by Sarah Kennedy

The Gold Thread by Sarah Kennedy

Rapture by Sarah Kennedy

Monster Zero by Jay Snodgrass

Drag by Duriel E. Harris

Running the Voodoo Down by Jim McGarrah

Assignation at Vanishing Point by Jane Satterfield

Her Familiars by Jane Satterfield

The Jewish Fake Book by Sima Rabinowitz

Recital by Samn Stockwell

Murder Ballads by Jake Adam York

Floating Girl (Angel of War) by Robert Randolph

Puritan Spectacle by Robert Strong

X-testaments by Karen Zealand

Keeping the Tigers Behind Us by Glenn J. Freeman

Bonneville by Jenny Mueller

State Park by Jenny Mueller

Cities of Flesh and the Dead by Diann Blakely

Green Ink Wings by Sherre Myers

Orange Reminds You Of Listening by Kristin Abraham

In What I Have Done & What I Have Failed To Do by Joseph P. Wood

Bray by Paul Gibbons

The Halo Rule by Teresa Leo

Perpetual Care by Katie Cappello

The Raindrop's Gospel: The Trials of St. Jerome and St. Paula by Maurya Simon

Prelude to Air from Water by Sandy Florian

Let Me Open You A Swan by Deborah Bogen

Cargo by Kristin Kelly

Spit by Esther Lee

Rag & Bone by Kathryn Nuernberger

Kingdom of Throat-stuck Luck by George Kalamaras

Mormon Boy by Seth Brady Tucker

Nostalgia for the Criminal Past by Kathleen Winter

Little Oblivion by Susan Allspaw

Quelled Communiqués by Chloe Joan Lopez

Stupor by David Ray Vance

Curio by John A. Nieves

The Rub by Ariana-Sophia Kartsonis

Visiting Indira Gandhi's Palmist by Kirun Kapur

Freaked by Liz Robbins

Looming by Jennifer Franklin

Flammable Matter by Jacob Victorine

Prayer Book of the Anxious by Josephine Yu

flicker by Lisa Bickmore

Sure Extinction by John Estes

Selected Proverbs by Michael Cryer

Rise and Fall of the Lesser Sun Gods by Bruce Bond

I will not kick my friends by Kathleen Winter

Barnburner by Erin Hoover

FICTION

How Things Break by Kerala Goodkin

Juju by Judy Moffat

Grass by Sean Aden Lovelace

Hymn of Ash by George Looney

Nine Ten Again by Phil Condon

Memory Sickness by Phong Nguyen

Troglodyte by Tracy DeBrincat

The Loss of All Lost Things by Amina Gautier

The Killer's Dog by Gary Fincke

Everyone Was There by Anthony Varallo

The Wolf Tone by Christy Stillwell